YESNO · DENNIS LEE

Dennis Lee

yesno

ANANSI

Published in 2007 by
House of Anansi Press Inc.
110 Spadina Avenue, Suite 801
Toronto, ON M5V 2K4
Tel. 416-363-4343
Fax 416-363-1017
www.anansi.ca

Distributed in Canada by
HarperCollins Canada Ltd.
1995 Markham Road
Scarborough, ON M1B 5M8
Toll free tel. 1-800-387-0117

10 09 08 07 06 1 2 3 4 5

Library and Archives Canada
Cataloguing in Publication

Lee, Dennis, 1939–
    Yesno : poems / Dennis Lee.

ISBN 978-0-88784-758-5

    I. Title.

PS8523.E3Y48 2007   C811'.54
    C2007-900068-1

We acknowledge for their financial
support of our publishing program
the Canada Council for the Arts,
the Ontario Arts Council, and the
Government of Canada through
the Book Publishing Industry
Development Program (BPIDP).

Printed and bound in Canada.

for Robert Bringhurst and Don McKay

CONTENTS

x

VI

If it walks like apocalypse. If it
squawks like armageddon.
If stalks the earth like anaphylactic parturition.
If halo jams like septicemic laurels, if
species recuse recuse if mutti clearcut, if
earth remembers how & then for good forgets.
If it glows like neural plague if it grins, if it
walks like apocalypse –

Combing the geo-pre-
frontal, scritch-
scratching for relicts of *yes*.

Giddyap, ganglia.

Skulldug, with sonic contusions.
Hushhammer riffs.

Here's to destiny chumps for a change.
Rogue arthurs; geek
parsifals; flammable joans of *salut*. To
insurrection gandhis.

Who but a bupkus
quixote would tilt at the corporate mindmills?
Who but a blunderling
underling hoot at the emperor's shanks?

Homeheart, great loanheart,
hang in;
blue planet, hold on.

Are scouts of the aquifer perilous –
ownheart, hang in.
Bog templars. Heroes of tall grass resumption;
geodyssey samurai.

Not fold, great homeheart,
hang in.
Hold hard in the septiclot thromb of extremis.

Walk soft, conquistador. Among your
teeming climes and species,
bwana, beware. No
brook is what it seems, nor
veldt, nor pampas.

Sahib, go slow,
tread light in the food-chain.
The cattle tick, the trout betray; sur-
veille the very air,
it stinks of ambush.

Bwana get back, the
stats are leaking!
Inside the palisade, chop-
chop your ownmost DNA is
flaunting injun spin.

And kiss your selves goodbye.
Is pasha crash, is
genghis melt is
its of you defecting.
No shelter.   *Pasaran*.

Blah-blah was easy, we
diddled the scrutable chunks;
whole hog was beyond us.

Bugspace &
chugspace ahead,
welcome wormlandia.

The birds con-
trive a nest. The wolves a lair.
Sheer matricide is rare.

Undernot rising. Bad
ом, the
holes in the wholly.

Bottleneck countdown; logomelt
cri du corps.
Stuck ruckus of geodilations.

What foetal botch impends? What
natal *awk*?
What gene-flubbed
cargo from postmark netherly?

And noful the species lacunae the alphazed shambles,
but yesward the clearwater improv & biogrit slog,
and noful the corporate borgias the aquagoth vaders,
but yesward the stewards emergent in homewhether stab,
and noful chromutant the decibel swoosh of warmwarning,
but yesward the jiminy wakeup to planetude lost –
and noful-but-yesward the herenow & bountyzip nowhere.

Pitch lumen. Crag
nadir. Sag tor.

Old icons go blank on the
dial, and the cumulo litter of *was*
exfoliates,
oliates,
oompahs the local to pulver.

How hew to the
pushpull? How
straddle the twain of what is?

Still singable
coleoptera. Still ozone
ave, still
redwoods memorious: earth

clamant, earth
keening earth
urnal, earth
gravid with loss.

Fluke
crusoe on boolean
sands, heart-
stopt with elderlore – still

spackled with
plosions of
let-there-be. *In-
cipit* afterplanet.

VII

Song sinister. Song
ligature; now
sing.
Are there honks, are there glyphs, are there
bare alingual grunts that
tonguefastly cleave to the judder of
habitat mending? the static of unsong un-
sung?

Dream on – of
bambino returning,
pox abated,
of scarified urchin-come-home.

Dream-on of bambino regained.
Wildward the
clearcut, oceans umbilical,
ozone declension on hold.

Bambino bambino, in
toxiholic recoil.
Escapist sanities.
Dreamfast, or nought.

As if a day more
diurnal, a night more
maternal, a planet more
chockful of plenum & wonders still dawdled ex
mammary/machina/magica,
poised for a last-real comeback.

Cold kaddish. In majuscule winter,
whistle down dixie to dusk;
coho with agave to dust.

Bison with orca commingled –
whistle down dixie. With
condor to audubon dust.

52 pickup, the species.
Beothuk, manatee, ash:
whistledown emu.

Vireo, mussel, verbena – cry
bygones, from heyday to dusk.
All whistling down dixie to dust.

Gene wranglers. Built
nature. Techgnosis.
Fresh necronyms of wild.

Weird ontoerotic ratios, plotting the
new by the new by the new by the new by the

Discarnate meanings mope . . . *Here
boy! Here boy!*
Someone will tend to them.

Someone will
tether them; christen them; shang-
bang them –

eros the psycho.

Mid-
mortem the greenly; mid-
greening the renaissant thud –
mixmatrix our motherland.

Grammars of outcome,
twin-
twined in collision/collusion.

In plenody, threnody, whenody,
snatches of
gracemare.

Bipsychopathways.
Ontonot denizen splat.

No DNA for the crunch – we got
neural nothing.
No yesno receptors; no template for cosmochaos.
No filter for earthly redamption.

Make me
cortical skootch in the trackless.
Amygdala vamp.

Sing me
synapse of hap and despire.

How surd a blurward stut. How
peewee thingsong,
surfing the plenary killcurve.

Barbary whoopup;
snatches of contact *ave.*

And borbo of cacohosanna: of smew of
beluga of animavegetal pibroch –
mixmuster of raggedy allsorts, syl-
labic in habitat soup.

Gumbo of
arkitude flotsam.
Flicker of
legacy toddlers, of
oldsoul avatar orphans.

Earth, you almost enough.
Hoof-high to excelsis, trilobite
sutra, cordillera jackpot:

into the new of attrition, the
birth of the lopped.
Into biosaudades.

Too fell a fate, green-
gone inheritor;
iotacome donner & ooze – still singing,

Hail to the unextinct,
oomph to the lorn-being-born.

VIII

Whacked grammar of terra
cognita. Old lingo
aphasic, nuworldspeak mute
mutant mutandis –
                    fumbumbling what
aleph? whose googoo? which syllab? Test-living what
schizoparse of *am*?

High whys of
lossolalia,
one blurt at a time.

Wildword the bounty extant.

Is earthscan in biscript, is
doublespeak goners-&-*hail*. Still itching to

parse with a two-tongued heart, shambala
scrapings. To
praise with a broken art.

Hope, you illicit
imperative: throw me a bone.
What sump, what gunge, what
sputter of sotto renewal?
What short shot
skitter of green reprise?

There is a fuse. A fuss. A flex of intent:
subsingular *is* on the hoof.
Radical larrup & given.

And it whiches, it
eachly enjoins.
Old dolittle spate.

To mark it, to
mark its incessance is
riteful as breathbone.

Halebent for
origin.
Creaturely mooch in the means.

And it falls like rain.
And it signifies like plague of indigenous nada.
And sluffs the everlocal yoke of *is*, while
gaga savants plot prosthetic fixes,
and noli tangos glide the lie fantastic, and
debit, debit, debit moans the moon –

telling how speakspace
puckers. How it
swivels and clots & ka-
boom! Percur-
vations in meanfield. Skewed
mentrics. Bunched losswaves. Impromptible knots of rebeing.
Rosetta palaver, unclued.

Test site, test
blight, to
whom now expiation?
In quantum
waste nirvana, what flawless
formulae forgive?

And avian farewells:
wordless in blinkerblank.
And nematode roads silting under:
hushmost palabras.
Cling to reverable, clang of no alibi, scrawk of un
uttered.
Of umbryo dicta, synching the lock-
jaw: (   ).

Crashable brainscape: not
crash. Exo-
skeletal whir of controls. Of
controls! Of skidlock, of some-
body-stop-us.

By pinsteps to choreocrackup.
Vertigo yen.

Courting the
glitch in the hominid regnum; craving slop-
stoppage of crash & blurn.

As stuttle inflex the genomes.
As bounty floundles.
As coldcock amnesia snakes thru
shoreline/sporelane/syngone –
                                        hi diddle
template, unning become us,
palimpsest gibber & newly.

I spin the yin stochastic, probble a
engram luff, & parse haw
bareback the whichwake, besoddle a thrashold flux.

Calling all
lords of the rigamort tango,
maestros of entropy glide:
we're pushing it
to with an amazon shimmy, hoofing it
fro with a greenhouse fandango; little bit
closer with canopy kissoffs, little bit
farther with coral abrasions –

Stepping lightly, cortex courageous,
high-hats macabre: keep keep keep
pumping that critterly whiteout, goosing it
faster in biophobe boogie;
doing the
gainful extinctions con carny, towing them
bones in the geospazz conga –

Last call for the
champs of demise now:
one more
glug of that sweet intifada, one more
slug of the rictus meringue,
treading the

rockabye samba to notown, strutting our
kamikaze victory obit –

Bellyful:
burnout is
best.

IX

You fold you are
folded, late-breaking primate, and
brought to who-knew.
Fold you are
null again, nil again, knell again – one-swat no-
see-um & whose. You
fold you are un:
stud of no
throne no dominion, kingshit of doodly.
Frag in the mean of let-be.

Earth heres, earth
nows, is there
nothing?

What whats?
Inlisten.
What blickens?

Inner than
polipulse, homer than breathbeat, listen to
isten. To

istence. Listen to *inguish*. Listen to
is.

What can, cog-
 nostic with earthwrack, be
(who?ishly) known to co-
here, co-now with the
ratiosacral flex of
original yes?

Deep
is, and be
struck. Be stricken.
Be amnioflex of the daily, as
things wriggle free of their names,
subsist in
sheer diggity *fiat*.

Be wild & be-
wildered.
Undermilk arbour, arbourmilk under:
sesame endwise.
Squiggles of *ing* on a
field of native null.

Herk lurch to
protobang:
quoti-
di/aeonic ah-
ha! What comes
to be is
beholden.

What we sniff/palp/schmeck/wrack/
ravish, but
can't commandeer. The
plosive being of beings.
Quickquark the ammonite, cognate the andes;
gratuitous stakeouts in time. Each a
fleck of first-day durance, a
fluxy reverb,
sheer chronojolt & onwards.

Thrum of material kickstart.
Fractals of genesis.

Baby come back. Come
easy come queasy come faraway-willaway,
bonehead electric like big boys but
baby come back, breathe
deep in the motherlode. Dumb
kopf in a sling & come broken;
baby come home.

Which thing is us.
We of the
waste-deep the
westering, we of the
cackabye outstinct on ice.

And are bodily implicates.
Are denizen-drenched, self-x'd,
are phyxiate foundlings,
woozy with birthright and
laced with caterwaul *rerum*.

Clamber down babel, climb down to the
nearaway country of homewhere. Of
bastard belong.

At the still open grave of the
not-yet-write-
offable cashcorpse –
blindblabbing our
gobshut, our
gutted-by-greenslag, our undisad-
missible burden: *for-*
gi-   *forgi-*

In morituri funk.

Body of primal, body of
plumb: it is to
you we owe our being,
carne of undergone aeons.

Destructible mother, survive us,
widewinnow our folly.
Foregather, in interlore
rehab agon, our
little, our lustral, our late.

X

Of more the less; of
least, prognostipangs.
Scrabbling for *abc*.

No heaven, no
beanstalk, bare earth.

Shedding what pyrotech-
tactics?
Threading what speakab/un-
speakable, ekable, seekable
gauntlet of need?

Terragon tilth, or
heartwork in kinderpolis.
To couch in the knit of the sinew, to
ponder refoliant scrub.
To gawp at what thrives without us.
To jimmy the civil equations, resetting for
osteo clicks of alignment,
onus upon us;
salaam to what heals
in the real.

Extempore if-
space & greening,
plant heartflag here.

Thru witslog, thru willslog to
glimmers of thingdom come;
pitch soulhold here.

Labour & claimstead – of
inchables,
karma oscura.

Staking the bundle. Brought,
broke, to
indigenous *fiat*.

Squeaks from the sisyphus chorus.
Hums from the crunch.
Dopey & grumpy & doc, just
truckin along –
here come chorale;
mind to the
grindstone, ear to the plough.

Hi-
hoein along with a song:
What home but here? Whose grubby hands but ours?

With a *yes*, with a *no*, with a
yesno:
sonics in simuljam.

To habitate crossbeing.
To ride both reals at once. To least-
wise stay
vif in detritus/un-
lulled by the blessingbait green.

If inly, if only, if
unly: heart-
iculate improv,
sussing the emes of what is.

Nor hunker in losslore, nor
kneejerk abracadaver.

Cripcryptic rejuice! Ec-
statisyllabic largesse –
rekenning, rekeening, re-
meaning our wordly demesne.

Grunts from the trench, the killzone:
peeps from the front.

Lithoslag / bioslag / noöslag –
hasta la omega.

Ciao to the caesarly, bye to the kaiserly, howdy
grim repo.

Hemis of brokensole. Demis. Mutt
angelus minims.

If hope disorders words, let
here be where.
Lingotectonics. Gondwana nar-
ruption vocale.

How can the
tonguetide of object/sub-
jection not garble what pulses in·
isbelly?

Nearflung & thingmost, re-
tuit sheer carnival logos. Where
nouns ignite
moves in the dance they denote:
moniker lifelines.
Cedarfast. Willowpang. Maplemind.
Oakable homing, notched in the bone.

Only co-
phonic. Co-
founded. Cofoundered.
Only galore.

Mercator cleanup or what?
Toxijam loosened, slum-
praxis goosed;
techmate relievo or what.

Alphas of stricken, bare omega noodlers –
swot to revivify human,
vamping on taptoes of *must*.

By the law by the lab by the ballot:
sanity sweat.
Lost-ditch endorphins or what.
Hometruth cojones. Or what?

Tell me, tall-
tell me a tale. The one about
starless & steerless & pinch-me, the
one about unnable now – which they did-did-
did in the plume of our pride, and
could not find the way home.
Little perps lost.

Yet a rescue appeared, in the
story a saviour arose. Called
limits. Called
duedate, called countdown ex-
tinction/collide. Called, eyeball to ego:
hubris agonistes.

Bad abba the endgame. In-
seminal doomdom alert:
pueblo naturans, or
else. But the breadcrumbs are gone, and the
story goes on, and how
haply an ending no
nextwise has shown us, nor known.

Dennis Lee has written twenty-one books, including the companion to this volume, *Un* (Anansi, 2003). His *Civil Elegies* won the Governor General's Literary Award, and his children's poetry is read around the world. He is also a noted essayist, song lyricist, and editor, and was the co-founder of Anansi in 1967. He lives in Toronto.

¶ Edited for the press by Don McKay and Ken Babstock.

Designed by Robert Bringhurst and set by Ingrid Paulson. The type is Van den Keere, a digital text family produced in the 1990s by Frank Blokland at the Dutch Type Library in The Hague. The roman is based on the work of the Flemish punchcutter Hendrik van den Keere (c.1540–1580) and the italic is the work of his French-born colleague François Guyot (c.1510–1570).

The photo of Dennis Lee on p 65 is by Susan Perly.

Yesno was completed with the assistance of the Canada Council.